YOUR KNOWLEDGE HAS VALUE

Temba Munsaka

The Importance of Project Feasibility Study

With practical examples

GRIN Verlag

Bibliografische Information der Deutschen Nationalbibliothek:

Die Deutsche Bibliothek verzeichnet diese Publikation in der Deutschen National-
bibliografie; detaillierte bibliografische Daten sind im Internet über http://dnb.d-
nb.de/ abrufbar.

Imprint:

Copyright © 2012 GRIN Verlag GmbH
Druck und Bindung: Books on Demand GmbH, Norderstedt Germany
ISBN: 978-3-656-53533-1

GRIN - Your knowledge has value

Der GRIN Verlag publiziert seit 1998 wissenschaftliche Arbeiten von Studenten, Hochschullehrern und anderen Akademikern als eBook und gedrucktes Buch. Die Verlagswebsite www.grin.com ist die ideale Plattform zur Veröffentlichung von Hausarbeiten, Abschlussarbeiten, wissenschaftlichen Aufsätzen, Dissertationen und Fachbüchern.

Visit us on the internet:

http://www.grin.com/

http://www.facebook.com/grincom

http://www.twitter.com/grin_com

TEMBA MUNSAKA

UD23301BPR31606

COURSE NAME: **"Project Feasibility & Selection: Discuss the importance of project feasibility study, giving practical examples"**

Student's Profile

Program: Doctorate of Project Management

ATLANTIC INTERNATIONAL UNIVERSITY

Table of Contents

Definition of Key Terms..3

Types of feasibility studies 4

Why a feasibility study in project management..5

Determining the profitability or viability of a project 6

Quantification of benefits and costs..6

Comparing of alternatives and selecting the best alternative...8

Identification of Target Beneficiaries 9

Finding out whether a project is needed 10

Designing a relevant marketing strategy..11

Identification of potential challenges or problems...11

Conclusion 12

References..13

Introduction

A feasibility study occupies a place of importance in contemporary project management. Decisions on whether to go ahead with a project and whether the intended beneficiaries will benefit from a project are informed by findings that emanate from a feasibility study. A feasibility study also helps project managers to determine whether a project is viable and select the best alternative from an array of alternatives that can address the identified problem. The feasibility study is one of the critical activities that are done at the first stage, the conceptualization phase of the project cycle. Therefore the feasibility study must be done meticulously so it generates appropriate and relevant information that will help project managers and stakeholders to make informed decisions on a given project. It must also be borne in mind that failure by the feasibility study to generate appropriate and relevant information may result in project managers making costly decisions that may impair the original intention or purpose of a project. This paper thus examines the importance of a feasibility study in project management.

Definition of Key Terms

Feasibility study: In the context of project management a feasibility study is a study that is done to determine options and whether the preferred or optimum option for a particular project is can achieve the desired objectives and sustainable given the likely resources available[1]. Feasibility study can also be defined as an analysis of the viability of an idea. The feasibility study focuses on helping answer the essential question of "should we proceed with the proposed project idea[2]?

Project: A project is any planned, temporary endeavor undertaken to create a unique product, service or other complete and definite outcome (deliverable) within a limited resource time scale and budget and normally requires mobilization of resources from different disciplines[3].

Project Management: Project management is the planning, organizing, directing and controlling of resources for a relatively short-term objective that has been established to

---

[1] US. Army Corps of Engineering, 2003:4.
[2] Micon International Limited, 2009:1
[3] Kerzner, H, 2011:14

complete specific goals and objectives[4]. Project management therefore can be described as the means, techniques and concepts used to run a project and achieve its objectives.

Types of feasibility studies

The importance of feasibility study in project management can only be understood within the context of the types of feasibility studies and their main focus. There are four types of feasibility studies. These four types are the technical, economic, schedule and operational feasibility[5]. Technical feasibility places particular focus on the availability of technology that is needed to achieve the objectives of the project[6]. The key considerations of technical feasibility are whether the technology is obtained locally, the costs of the technology if it is to be imported and how relevant is it to the achievement of project objectives. In a broad sense technical feasibility seeks to determine the availability, costs and technological risks associated with technology that is needed to achieve project objectives. For example technologically intense projects such as mining require a detailed technical feasibility study that will determine technological availability, costs and associated risks particularly to the environment.

Economic feasibility studies focus on the costs associated with a project and how they can be kept at a minimum level[7]. The major factor under an economic feasibility study is whether the project is possible given the resource constraints. Economic feasibility seeks to determine the monetary benefits that accrue from a given project as well as the financial costs associated with a project. Usually a project alternative that yields more benefits than costs is adopted and implemented[8]. For instance in a dam construction project, if an alternative promises to give more benefits in terms of the number of irrigation schemes that will benefit the local people, returns from possible tourism ventures and envisaged drinking water security there is a high possibility that it will be adopted. However, in developing countries such as Zimbabwe projects are selected not on the basis of the results of an economic

[4] Kerzner, H, 2011:15
[5] Harrington, R, 2011:2
[6] Ibid, p4
[7] Wysocki, R.K and McGary, R, 2008:5
[8] Carley, M, 1987:10

feasibility study but on the basis of political mileage that they will yield to the governing elites[9].

A schedule feasibility study seeks to determine whether it is possible to develop a solution within reasonable time and the time frame needed to implement the selected alternative to achieve project objectives[10]. In broad terms, schedule feasibility is preoccupied with arranging the key project activities and determining whether they can be achieved within the allotted time frame. The aim is to avoid unnecessary delays that may increase the cost of the project or delay benefit to the intended beneficiaries[11]. In the construction of stadiums and related facilities for major world events such as the Olympics games time schedules are of critical importance. The stadiums have to be completed within a given time frame if the games are to be held successfully. Thus schedule feasibility is needed to determine project completion within a set time frame.

Feasibility studies are also in the form of operational feasibility. Operational feasibility places emphasis on the system that will be activated to achieve project objectives[12]. In the context of operational feasibility an operational system is a process that brings together collaboration between the human, materials, financial resources in order to achieve project objectives[13]. Utilization of human, material and financial resources needs to be done in a systematic manner so that the project activities and objectives are achieved at minimum cost as well as within a set time frame. Operational feasibility study provides solutions as to how project resources can be synchronized so that project objectives are achieved timely. Countries such as Brazil hosting the Olympic games in 2016 need to carry out operational feasibility studies so that there is effective utilization of resources to timely complete projects such as stadiums that will host the games.

Why a feasibility study in project management

There are several compelling reasons why it is of critical importance to carry out a feasibility study in project management. Since a project is a one off event, which is unlikely to be repeated, project managers need to be equipped with appropriate and relevant facts that help

---

[9] Ibid, p22.
[10] Caranci, M.J and Wideman, K, 2011:6.
[11] Ibid, p7.
[12] University of Toronto, 2009
[13] Overton, R 2007

them determine whether to go ahead or abandon the project all together[14]. Such critical decisions can only be taken on the basis of information that comes out from a feasibility study. Logically this part of the paper is going to discuss the importance of feasibility studies in project management.

Determining the profitability or viability of a project

The importance of a feasibility study in project management probably more than anything else lies in determining whether a project is profitable and worthwhile to implement[15]. Feasibility studies in project management provide significant information on whether a project is profitable in the short and long term. Profitability projections made by the project managers show the profit margins that the project is set to generate in all the key phases of inception. Whether a project is viable or profitable is of critical importance to all the stakeholders to a project. Investment decisions by shareholders are informed by the profitability and viability trends that are generated by a feasibility study[16]. The decision by a company to expand its network coverage through the construction of more base stations'is directly influenced by the projected profits that are associated with such a venture both in the short and long term. Consequently, most projects are assessed on the basis of their projected profitability and viability. Those projects that show favorable profitability projections are usually adopted and implemented. Profitability is usually assessed by comparing the envisaged benefits and costs. The higher the benefits than costs, it is most likely that the project will be adopted.

Quantification of benefits and costs

The importance of the feasibility study in project management lies in its ability to quantifying benefits and costs associated with a project. Quantification of benefits and costs in project management is done using the cost benefit analysis (CBA) technique[17]. Practically, CBA can be better understood from the background of the scarcity of resources where an attempt is made in any choice situation to arrive to a decision that make the best use of those limited

---

[14] Scottish Community Project Fund, 2009.
[15] Overton, R, 2007:15.
[16] Turner, J.R, 2009:5
[17] Geoff, R, 2011: 7.

resources at the disposal of project managers. CBA is defined as a technique for assessing the monetary social costs and benefits of a capital investment project over a given time period[18]. Thus drawing from the foregoing definition, CBA as a rational empirical technique seeks to quantify all the relevant factors that guide a decision by expressing the potential alternatives in monetary terms. Specific measures are developed for projects' anticipated benefits and costs and the ratio of costs to benefits could be computed as well as the net project benefit on whose basis a choice of the best alternative is made[19]. Of paramount importance is the fact that CBA assesses whether a project offers a positive net economic return to society at large or not and also evaluates alternative means of achieving a specific objective. Further the CBA is quite useful in determining the spillover impact of projects which is crucial to project managers concerned with both unintended and intended consequences of projects[20]. Apart from its utility as a decision tool technique which assists decision makers to make informed decisions and gain insights of the consequences of their decisions, it also serves as a monitoring tool for the decisions made.

Invariably, CBA is guided by the principles of appraisal of a project, incorporation of externalities and discounting[21]. Appraisal of a project is an economic technique for project appraisal, widely used in business as well as government spending projects. For example should a business invest in a new information system? CBA incorporates externalities into the equation, it can, if required, include wider social and environmental impacts as well as 'private' economic costs and benefits so that externalities are incorporated into the decision process[22]. In this way, CBA can be used to estimate the social welfare effects of a project. Time matters in CBA. CBA can take account of the economics of time – known as discounting. This is important when looking at environmental impacts of a project in the years ahead.

However, quantification of benefits and costs is not an easy and straight forward feasibility study activity. It is difficult to quantify social costs and benefits associated with a project[23]. This presents a challenge to project managers when carrying out a feasibility study. For example it is hard to quantify loss of a natural habitat by a group of people such as the Tonga

---

[18] Gramlich, E.D, 1990: 14.
[19] Gramlich, E.D, 1990:20.
[20] Elgar, E, 1996:10
[21] Cohen,H, et al, 1996:13
[22] Ibid, p14
[23] Greenberg, et al 2001:6

people who were displaced during the construction of the Kariba dam in the 1950s along the Zambezi River. Up to this day the social costs incurred by the Tonga people as a result of the Kariba dam project is not known. Evidence on the ground reveal that the Kariba dam project has irreparably disrupted the socio-cultural life of the Batonga people as they now found themselves separated into two nationalities (Zimbabwean and Zambian) which was not the case before the construction of the dam. The Kariba dam project thus shades insight into how a feasibility study can fail to quantify some costs and benefits which have direct influence on social groups directly affected by a project.

Comparing of alternatives and selecting the best alternative

Project management entails comparison of alternatives and the feasibility study enables project managers to compare project alternatives[24]. It is important to compare project alternatives before selecting the most feasible alternative that will achieve the envisaged project objectives. This is only possible through a feasibility study. Techniques such as the CBA are applied to compare project alternatives. Usually in comparing project alternatives project managers consider the benefits and costs associated with each alternative. Timing is very critical in comparing benefits and costs of a project. The costs and benefits estimated occur unevenly over many years. Thus CBA takes this timing of costs and benefits into account through the process referred to as discounting. This technique reduces the face value of future benefits to reflect the idea that time is valuable.

However, it is imperative to note that the selection of the discount rate is the trickiest part of the process since the higher the discount rate the lower the value of project and vice versa thereby distorting the economic estimate of the alternative[25]. The results of the discounting procedure is the bottom line economic estimate that a decision maker looks for in a cost-benefit analysis usually the estimated annual flows of CBA are summarised as Net Present Value (NPV), Benefit Cost Ratios, Internal Rate of Return (IRR). Usually an alternative with a high NPV/Benefit cost Ratio or IRR is the first choice if there are more than one alternative. If there is one alternative, it is selected when the bottom line economic estimate is positive and vice versa.

---

[24]Greenberg, G ,et al, 2001:17.
[25] Elgar, R, 1996:5.

Identification of Target Beneficiaries

Feasibility study in project management helps project managers to identify target beneficiaries as well as groups of people that may be affected by the project[26]. By their nature projects are undertaken to benefit targeted beneficiaries. The feasibility study serves the purpose of identifying the groups of people that stand to benefit from a project and the possible extent to which they are likely to benefit[27]. Failure to identify target beneficiaries may lead to project failing to achieve its objective or failing to serve its original intended purpose. A project such as the construction of a new clinic requires a detailed feasibility study that will determine the number of people in an area so that the health facility can be positioned strategically. The feasibility study help the distance people travel to access the health services. This means for the feasibility study to identify the target beneficiaries community wide consultations have to be done. These consultations will not only help the project managers to identify the target beneficiaries but will also reveal how these beneficiaries want to benefit from the project.

In business, projects such as the launch of a new product require a feasibility study that will identify the segments of the market that will likely purchase the product. Once the feasibility study identifies the target beneficiaries it is easy for the project managers to modify or tailor make a product in accordance with the preferences of the target beneficiaries. Identification of the target beneficiaries through the feasibility study helps project managers to determine how they are to deploy resources from a technical, economic and operational standpoint. For example when Econet decided to expand its network coverage their feasibility study pointed out that the majority of the people in Zimbabwe are in the rural areas. To capture this segment of the market which was underserved in terms of network coverage there was need to construct more base stations in the rural areas. The result was phenomenal increase in the subscribers which translated to increased revenues for Econet.

Identification of target beneficiaries through the feasibility study has its own challenges. Projects aimed at targeting people with HIV have faced challenges given the stigma attached to the disease. Self-help projects such as nutrition gardens in rural Zimbabwe have failed to benefit genuine beneficiaries as those infected with HIV fear to come out in the open for fear of being marginalized in the wider society on their grounds of their condition because of the

---

[26]Mitchell, R.K, et al, 1997:5.
[27] Schwager, H.P, 2004:7

stigma associated with the disease[28]. Even in business related projects it is not easy to identify the target beneficiaries of a project. Consumer preferences change and this distorts the identification of the target beneficiaries. For the economic crisis of the past decade in Zimbabwe has drastically altered the preferences of the consumers. To establish the authentic target beneficiaries a feasibility study has to be thorough so that it captures the underlying dynamics that can mask the genuine beneficiaries of a project.

Finding out whether a project is needed

The importance of a feasibility study in project management is its ability to reveal whether a project or product is needed by the target beneficiaries and whether they are willing to spend on the product[29]. It is critical that project managers should know that their intended project or product is needed by the segment of the population targeted as well the magnitude to which that population is prepared to spend on the product. For example project managers have to ascertain whether motorists really need blend petrol so that the biofuel project can be scaled up into a full-fledged commercial venture. Knowledge of whether a project is needed can influence investment decisions and provide useful insight into whether a project is commercially viable. The low uptake of blend petrol by the Zimbabwean motoring public reveal the limitations of failing to carry out a detailed feasibility study[30]. This has affected the biofuel (ethanol project) in the Chisumbanje area in South Eastern Zimbabwe, potentially threatening the livelihoods of thousands of workers who had become reliant on the project for survival. If a proper feasibility study was carried out project managers could have gathered sufficient information on whether blend petrol is needed by the motoring public and may be devised ways to create an interest in the motoring public if demand for it was perceived to be low as is the case currently. Thus this shows that the feasibility study is an important aspect of project management as it provides information that can influence the decision to go ahead or abandon a given project.

---

[28] Sunday Mail September 2011.
[29] Alwang, J, et al, 2003:4
[30] Sunday Mail Septemper 2012

Designing a relevant marketing strategy

A feasibility study helps project managers to devise appropriate marketing strategies to capture the intended target groups[31]. In the implementation of projects in the business fraternity it is essential that a feasibility study should provide information that will help project managers to design relevant marketing strategies that will capture the desired market segment. This will mean that cost effective marketing strategies will be developed that reduce costs and maximize the market reach that promote the sale of the new product. For example project managers overseeing the production of a new mobile phone brand have to carry out a feasibility study that will help them create a market niche in a market that is traditionally dominated by time tested brands such as Nokia, Samsung and Blackberry. Thus the feasibility study provides critical information that shapes the marketing strategy so that a project meets its set objectives at minimum cost.

Identification of potential challenges or problems

Apart from helping project managers assess whether a project is viable the feasibility study also serve the purpose of identifying potential challenges or problems associated with a project[32]. The development of a project is a highly complex exercise which is fraught with many challenges or problems. Any well-meaning project manager has to have an in-depth knowledge of these challenges so that measures can be developed to circumvent these challenges. Challenges present themselves in different forms. They could be technological challenges that come as a result of technological deficiencies[33]. For example in the creation of a new product such as an energy efficient vehicle technological challenges come in the form of lack of a scientific formula that can lead to the development of an engine that converts fuel in a way that is energy efficient. As is the present case scientists are locked up in a battle to try and generate a scientific formula that will replace petrol and diesel engines in their quest to develop an energy efficient vehicle.

Challenges can be of an operational nature. Operational challenges are those challenges that are associated with limitations imposed by lack of adequate systems that promote the efficient, effective and economic coordination of project resources namely human, financial,

---

[31] Thompson, A.A, et al, 2010:15.
[32] Thompson Jr, A.A, 2006:6
[33] Ibid, p8.

and material resources[34]. It must be noted that organization or operational challenges can affect the achievement of project as lack of proper planning, organization; leading and control can harm the smooth implementation of project activities.

It must also be noted that challenges can be in the form of economic challenges. Economic challenges can be in the form of inflation which affect the procurement as well as the availability of project resources[35]. In an inflationary environment the prices of resources tend to rise drastically and this can offset scheduling of the project activities. In the period 2004 to 2008 Zimbabwe experienced an episode of economic crisis characterized by hyperinflation this affected the completion of projects such as the dualisation of major highways.

Conclusion

From the above discussion the feasibility study is of critical importance in project management. Before a project is implemented it has to be ascertained whether it is viable, needed by the target beneficiaries and sustainable. The potential challenges that may affect the project need to be known so that measures can be put in place to circumvent them. Thus broadly conceptualized, a feasibility study is of critical importance if projects are to achieve set objectives.

---

[34] Ibid, p17
[35] Bryson, J.M, 1988:8

12

References

Alwang, J, et al Why has poverty increased in Zimbabwe Washington DC, World Bank, 2003.

Bryson, J.M, Strategic Planning for Public and Nonprofit Organizations. Oxford: Jossey-Bass Publishers, 1988.

Caranci, M. J and Wideman , K, Rating Project Finance Methodology, Toronto, DBRS, 2011

Carley, M. Rational Techniques in Policy Analysis. London Crower 1987.

Cohen, H, et al (1996) An Introduction to Cost and Benefit Approach to Social Programs, National Institute of Justice, Washington D.C.

Elgar, E. (1996) Applied Cost-Benefit Analysis, National Institute of Justice, Washington D.C.

Geoff ,R CBA in Practice [Accessed 14 October 2012 (www.about.com).

Gramlich, E, D. A Guide to Benefit-Cost Analysis, New Jersey Prentice-Hall, 1990.

Greenberg, A. R. et al Cost-Benefit Analysis :Concepts and Practice. Prentice Hall, 2001.

Harrington, R Practical Project Management Techniques How to make money and get ahead in the video world www.RichardHarringtonBlog.com (Accessed 7 October 2012).

Kerzner, H. Project-Based Metrics, KPIs and Dashboards , London, John Wiley & Sons, 2011.

Micon International Limited , Feasibility Studies and Project Management, London, MIL, 2009

Mitchell, R.K., Agle B.R. and Wood, D.J. 'Toward a theory of stakeholder identification and salience: defining the principle of who and what really counts'. Academy of Management Review. 22(4), 1997.

Overton , R Feasibility Studies Made Simple , Boat Harbour, Martin Books Pty Ltd, 2007.

Schwager, H. P, Organizational strategies to address stakeholder relationships : A customer perspective portal PhD thesis Aubum University, 2004.

Scottish Community Project Fund, Feasibility Studies : A Guide to Good Practice RIAS Edinburgh, 2004.

Sunday Mail September 2011.

Thompson, A.A., Strickland,A.J., Gamble, J.E. Crafting and Executing Strategy. New York ,McGraw Hill, 2010.

Thompson Jr, A. S. Crafting and Executing Strategy, The Quest for Competitive Advantage. New York. McGraw-Hill companies, 2006.

Turner, J. R. The Handbook of Project Based Management: Leading Strategic Change in Organizations, New York, McGraw-Hill, 2009.

U.S. Army Corps of Engineers, Project Management Plan Grand Calumet Feasibility Study Chicago District, 2003.

University of Toronto Feasibility Studies , Toronto, 2010

Wysocki, R. K and McGary, R Effective Project Management: Traditional, Adaptive, Extreme 3rd Edition, 2008.